WITHDRAWN

★ IT'S MY STATE! ★

Pennsylvania

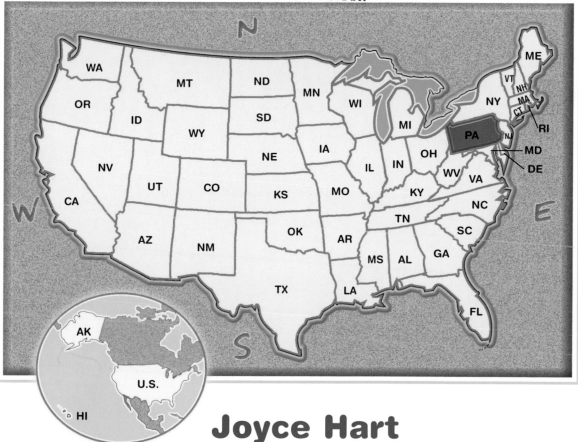

Joyce Hart

BENCHMARK BOOKS

MARSHALL CAVENDISH
NEW YORK

Series Consultant

David G. Vanderstel, Ph.D., Executive Director, National Council on Public History

With thanks to Laura Tuennerman-Kaplan, Ph.D., Assistant Professor in the Department of History and Political Science, California University of Pennsylvania, for her expert review of the manuscript.

Benchmark Books
Marshall Cavendish Corporation
99 White Plains Road
Tarrytown, New York 10591-9001
www.marshallcavendish.com

Text, maps, and illustrations copyright © 2004 by Marshall Cavendish Corporation
Map and illustrations by Christopher Santoro

Hart, Joyce, 1954–
Pennsylvania / by Joyce Hart
p. cm. — (It's my state!)
Summary: Surveys the history, geography, government, and economy of
Pennsylvania, as well as the diverse ways of life of its people.
Includes bibliographical references and index.
ISBN 0-7614-1691-9
1. Pennsylvania—Juvenile literature. [1. Pennsylvania.] I. Title. II. Series.

F149.3.H37 2004
974.8—dc22
2003020341

Photo research by Candlepants, Inc.

Front cover: Joe McDonald / Corbis

Back cover: The license plate shows Pennsylvania's postal abbreviation, followed by its year of statehood.

Corbis: 29, 54, 60; Pat O'Hara, 4 (bottom); Kevin Schafer, 5 (middle); Bob Krist, 8, 40, 62, 68 (bottom); Joe McDonald, 10; W. Cody, 13; George D. Lepp, 17 (middle); D. Robert & Lorri Franz, 20; Bettmann, 22, 31, 35, 37, 48 (top), 48 (middle), 49 (bottom); Medford Historical Society Collection, 36; Archivo Iconografico, S.A., 39 (top); Lester Lefkowitz, 39 (bottom); Ted Spiegel, 46, 52; Sygma, 48 (bottom); Francis G. Mayer, 49 (middle); Underwood & Underwood, 49 (top); Lee Snider, 56; Richard T. Nowitz, 58, 67; David Zimmerman, 66; Michael Pole, 68 (top); Tim Wright, 68 (middle); Matthias Kulka, 69 (top); Joel Sartore, 69 (bottom); Catherine Karnow, 73. *AnimalsAnimals / Earth Scenes:* McDonald Wildlife Photography, 4 (middle), 19; Michael Gadomski, 14, 15; Ted Levin, 16 (middle); Erwin & Peggy Bauer, 17 (top); Barbara von Hoffmann, 18. *Photo Researchers, Inc.:* Michael P. Gadomski, 4 (top); J. White, 5 (top); Scott-Berthoule, 16 (top); Darwin Dale, 16 (bottom); Richard Parker, 17(bottom); Jeffrey Lepore, 21. *Commonwealth Media Center:* Brig Niagara, 5 (bottom). *SuperStock:* Vernon Sigl, 9; Richard Cummins, 11. *The Bridgeman Art Library:* Private Collection, 25; Atwater Kent Museum of Philadelphia/Courtesy of Historical Society of Pennsylvania Collection, Atwater Kent Museum of Philadelphia, 27; Pennsylvania State Capitol, PA, USA, 32.*John McGrail Photography:* 42. *Peter Johannes / Ravenwood Studios:* 43. *The Image Works:* Mark Ludak, 47, 51, 72; David Wells, 50. *Diane Meyer:* 53. *Envision:* Steven Needham, 64; Paul Poplis, 69 (middle).*Index Stock Imagery:* Rudi Von Briel, 65; Mark Gibson, 71. *Robertstock:* J. Irwin, 74.

Printed in Italy

1 3 5 6 4 2

Contents

A Quick Look at Pennsylvania

Nickname: Keystone State

Population: 12,287,150 (2001 estimate)

Satehood: December 12, 1787

Tree: Hemlock

The hemlock is an evergreen tree that can grow up to two hundred feet tall. It thrives in almost every area of Pennsylvania and was popular with early settlers. The settlers used the wood to build their wagons, cabins, and furniture.

Bird: Ruffed Grouse

The ruffed grouse is a reddish brown bird. A grouse can grow to be about 20 inches long with a wingspan of about 20 inches. These plump birds spend a lot of time on the ground, making them easy for hunters to find. Many early inhabitants of Pennsylvania used the grouse for food.

Flower: Mountain Laurel

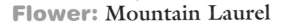

The Pennsylvania legislature could not decide between choosing the honeysuckle or the mountain laurel as the state flower. In 1933 the choice was left to the wife of Governor Gifford Pinchot. Mrs. Pinchot selected the mountain laurel, a woodland shrub with white and pink blossoms that grows in Pennsylvania forests.

Dog: Great Dane

Brought over from England, Great Danes were very popular with early settlers. This is because they are very good hunting and guard dogs. In 1965 the state legislature honored the Great Dane's strength and loyalty by making it Pennsylvania's official dog. A portrait of William Penn together with his Great Dane hangs in the governor's reception room in Harrisburg.

Fossil: *Phacops rana*

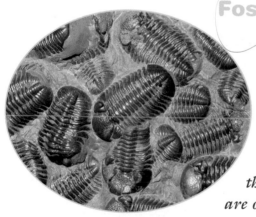

Over three hundred million years ago, most of Pennsylvania was underwater. As a result, many of the state's fossils are sea creatures, such as the Phacops rana. This creature was a kind of trilobite. Trilobites were the ancestors of crabs and spiders and were among the first living things on earth known to have eyes. Trilobite fossils are often found in Pennsylvania.

Flagship: U.S. Brig *Niagara*

This large warship was involved in the Battle of Lake Erie, an 1813 fight between the United States and Great Britain. The fight was part of the War of 1812. The original U.S. Brig Niagara eventually sank, but was raised and reconstructed in 1913 and is now on display at the port in Erie, Pennsylvania.

1 The Keystone State

Located in the eastern portion of the United States, Pennsylvania has a varied landscape. Powerful geological forces created the different land features. According to geological theories, millions of years ago tectonic plates, found beneath the surface of the earth, shifted and crashed into each other. This activity formed mountain chains across parts of North America. Volcanoes and earthquakes further changed the landscape. Then, about ten thousand years ago, huge masses of ice covered most of North America. This included the northern portion of present-day Pennsylvania. As the glaciers—slow-moving masses of ice—moved northward, rivers, valleys, and lakes were carved into the earth. Through the years, wind, water, and other natural forces have continued to shape Pennsylvania into the land it is today. As a result, Pennsylvania's landscape includes flat plains, gently rolling hills, valleys, and steep mountain chains.

Pennsylvania's Borders
North: New York and Lake Erie
South: Delaware, Maryland, and West Virginia
East: New York and New Jersey
West: Ohio

The Landscape

The flat land in the northwestern corner of the state is called the Great Lakes Plain. This plain hugs the shores of Lake Erie. Lake Erie is one of the five Great Lakes and is the twelfth-largest lake in the world. The Great Lakes Plain is a relatively flat strip of land. In this region you will find the city of Erie. With a little over 100,000 people, this city is the state's major port on the lake.

The edge of the plain gives way to a high plateau. A plateau is a mass of land that rises above the land surrounding it. The sides of a plateau often look like steep walls. Some plateaus are flat on the

Visitors and residents can swim, boat, and hike through Presque Isle State Park situated along Lake Erie.

Located in the Tioga State Forest, the 47-mile-long Grand Canyon of Pennsylvania is home to magnificent rock formations and state parks.

top, but the Appalachian Plateau, sometimes called the Allegheny Plateau, has a rather rugged top that is covered with forests. The Appalachian Plateau covers most of the western and northern portions of the state. Today there are many state parks and national forests located on the Appalachian Plateau, but there is little human settlement here. The plateau region is famous, however, for its rich deposits of coal and oil.

The Appalachian Plateau gradually increases in height and becomes part of the Appalachian Mountains. The Appalachian Mountain range is a large chain of mountains that runs from southeastern Canada down to central Alabama. Many geologists believe that the Appalachian Mountain range is one of the oldest mountain ranges in the world. It has been calculated that about 200 million years ago the Appalachian Mountains were over 15,000 feet high. Through the years, however, earthquakes and volcanic activity changed the features of the mountains. Glaciers that moved through the area during the Ice Age further eroded—or wore away—the mountain peaks. Rain and wind continued to eat away at the mountains, leveling them to their current elevations.

The portion of the Appalachians that runs through Pennsylvania is called the Allegheny Mountains. Pittsburgh is located in the northern foothills of the Alleghenies. It is Pennsylvania's second–largest city and has a population of more than 300,000 people. The highest point in Pennsylvania is Mount Davis. Located in southern Pennsylvania amid the Alleghenies, this peak stands 3,213 feet high.

The Alleghenies give way to a series of smaller mountain ranges: the Jacks, the Tuscarora, and the Blue mountains. These ranges are located in an area that is referred to as the Great Valley region. The state capital, Harrisburg, is located in the Great Valley region.

Moving eastward from the Alleghenies and the Great Valley region, the land flattens out. The land becomes level at the Piedmont Plateau. The Piedmont extends from Pennsylvania

Crop farms and livestock ranches thrive in Pennsylvania's fertile regions.

into New Jersey and Maryland, and continues south toward Alabama. The Pennsylvanian portion of the Piedmont Plateau is not as rugged as the Appalachian Plateau. In Pennsylvania the Piedmont is a landscape of rolling hills and fertile soil. Because the soil is ideal for crops, many of Pennsylvania's farms are located in the Piedmont. The city of Lancaster, with a population of a little more than 56,000 people, is located in the Pennsylvania Piedmont.

At the southeastern corner of the state you will find the Atlantic Coastal Plain. The full Atlantic Coastal Plain stretches down the southern edge of the United States from New York

The bustling city of Philadelphia lies along the edge of the Schuylkill River.

to Florida. Like the Great Lakes Plain, the land of the Atlantic Coastal Plain is mostly very flat and very fertile. This coastal plain is home to Philadelphia, Pennsylvania's largest city. The Delaware River makes up part of the southeastern border of the state, separating Pennsylvania from New Jersey.

The Waterways

Pennsylvania has many bodies of water. Several lakes dot the state. Some are natural lakes formed over years of geologic change. Others are artificial lakes, created to keep Pennsylvania's rivers from flooding. Pennsylvania's largest natural lake is Conneaut Lake in the northwestern part of the state.

Many rivers flow through the mountains, creating some of the most beautiful waterfalls on the East Coast. The major rivers in the state include the Delaware in the east, the Susquehanna in the center of the state, and the Ohio in the west. Water sports such as fishing, canoeing, and white-water rafting are very popular in Pennsylvania's waters.

The rivers of Pennsylvania also provided a major means of transportation for many years. Their usefulness was increased by a series of man-made canals that were constructed as early as 1797. These canals connected rivers and allowed people and cargo to travel over land features such as parts of the Alleghenies. Large floods have destroyed some canals, but historical markers point out where many of the canals were dug.

The Climate

Pennsylvania enjoys four distinct weather seasons. The average temperature in the winter is about 30 degrees Fahrenheit.

While Pennsylvania's streams, lakes, and rivers are good for outdoor sports, the state's waterfalls are perfect for those who want to simply enjoy the state's natural beauty.

Pennsylvania's winters bring freezing temperatures, cold winds, and sometimes heavy snowfall.

Sometimes the temperature drops below zero, especially in the mountains. The northern and western parts of Pennsylvania are usually colder in the winter than the southern and eastern portions. Pennsylvania winters also bring snow and ice.

In the spring, temperatures begin to warm up. This season can also include heavy rainfall. By June, summer temperatures usually rise to the sixties and seventies. Besides high temperatures, the summer also brings humidity. The big cities, like Philadelphia, can become the hottest places in July and August. But as fall approaches, temperatures quickly cool down.

Wildlife

At one time Pennsylvania was covered with forests. As European settlers came to the state, many trees were cut down to build houses, furniture, and wagons. The forests also supplied wood to keep the settlers warm and to cook their food. As the population grew, more land was cleared in order to create farmland for crops and livestock. The lumber industry thrived in Pennsylvania during the 1800s and 1900s. By the 1900s, several forests had been completely destroyed. But in the last 150 years, residents have been working very hard to restore their forests. Today Pennsylvania has over 17 million acres of woods.

The leaves of the trees in this hardwood forest in the Pocono Mountains change color with the shifting seasons.

Plants & Animals

Brook Trout

Brook trout can be found in Pennsylvania's cool lakes and streams. These trout are very colorful fish, with light green backs highlighted with yellow and black spots. They are the only fish native to Pennsylvania. The brook trout is Pennsylvania's official state fish.

Great Blue Heron

The great blue heron is the largest member of the heron family. This bird stands almost three feet tall and is an excellent fisher. It catches its food by wading in shallow water, then waiting patiently without moving until a fish swims by. Once it sees a fish, it slowly folds its long neck back, then quickly plunges its head into the water and catches the fish with its long, sharp beak.

Firefly

On summer nights, most fields and forests in Pennsylvania are filled with the blinking lights of fireflies. Scientists believe that a firefly—which is also the state's official insect—has two uses for its flashing light: to scare away creatures that might want to eat it and to attract a mate.

Striped Skunk

Striped skunks live in forests and near farmland. They eat insects, fruits, plants, and sometimes mice. Skunks are bushy tailed and black, with bold white stripes running down their backs. When frightened or threatened, these little creatures release a very strong scent that most animals—including humans—cannot stand.

Blackberries

Blackberry bushes grow wild in the mountainous regions of Pennsylvania. Their long branches are covered with thorns and create hedges of tangled brambles. These offer great hiding places for small forest creatures. In the spring, blackberry flowers bloom, and in the late summer the sweet fruit grows on the branches.

Slippery Elm

Pennsylvania has over one hundred different species—or types—of native trees, and the slippery elm is one of them. Slippery elm is about 60 feet tall. The wood is sometimes used to make furniture. The inner bark of the tree has been used for many hundreds of years as a medicine. Early Native Americans used elm bark to build canoes.

Forested and woodland areas are a raccoon's natural habitat, but more are moving closer to suburban or urban areas.

These forests are home to trees such as maple, oak, birch, pine, and elm. In the fall, Pennsylvania forests and hills turn lovely shades of orange, red, and yellow as the leaves change colors. Flowers bloom alongside the trees. Pennsylvania's state flower, the mountain laurel, grows wild in the forests, as do azaleas and rhododendrons. All three of these plants are flowering bushes that bloom in the late spring. There are also many sweet fruits growing naturally in Pennsylvania. They include wild blackberries, raspberries, and elderberries. Plants and fruits such as these provide homes and food for the wild animals that live in Pennsylvania.

Pennsylvania

Pennsylvania's forests and fields are home to rabbits, raccoon, opossums, deer, squirrels, and bats. On a nature hike, visitors to the state might also spot beavers, minks, woodchucks, and chipmunks. Black bears and bobcats were once almost extinct in the state, but their numbers are increasing.

The state is also home to many different types of birds. There are also plenty of wild turkeys and ruffed grouse. Ducks, geese, and herons are often around the state's waterways. Robins, sparrows, larks, chickadees, owls, hawks, and falcons may be seen in the skies or perched in the trees.

Four young screech owls huddle together on a branch near their nests. As they get older, the owls' feathers become smoother and appear less fluffy.

A male elk—called a bull—rests in this Pennsylvania field.

Endangered Wildlife in Pennsylvania

Many species of plants and animals that lived in the state hundreds or thousands of years ago are no longer around. This is mostly because of human settlement in the region. To make way for civilization, forests were cut down and waterways were rerouted, destroying the natural homes and food for many animals. Overhunting and pollution have also affected certain animal species.

Elk have twice become almost extinct in the Allegheny Mountains. But thanks to conservation efforts, today Pennsylvania is proud of the fact that the state has some of the largest herds east of the Mississippi River.

Bald eagles used to fly across Pennsylvania skies and nest in the tall trees. But for most of the twentieth century, there were no bald eagles left in the state. Laws were passed restricting people from harming these eagles. Conservation efforts to breed and release these striking birds began. As a result, the populations have slowly begun to increase. Today you might see bald eagles living in forested areas around the Delaware and Susquehanna rivers. This is just one example of how Pennsylvanians are working to protect their land and the wildlife on it.

Patient birdwatchers might be able to see a majestic bald eagle soaring over some of Pennsylvania's rivers.

2 From the Beginning

Pennsylvania has a rich and interesting history, created by the different people who have lived on the land: the Native Americans, English, Dutch, Swedish, Americans, and the people who live there now. Their experiences and influences have shaped the state into what it is today.

Native American History

Anthropologists—scientists who study past human life and activities—estimate that humans have lived in Pennsylvania for approximately 16,000 years. The first people to inhabit the area lived in small tribes. They did not build permanent homes and traveled from place to place hunting and gathering food along the way. These people most likely moved with the seasons. In the summer, they might have lived near the rivers where they could catch fish. In the fall, they probably moved toward the mountains, where they ate wild berries, nuts, and other plants and animals that grew there. In the winter they probably hunted bigger animals that lived in the mountains.

Three champion marble shooters compete at a tournament in Philadelphia in 1926.

23

As time passed, some of the tribes built more permanent villages, mostly along Pennsylvania's major rivers such as the Susquehanna. These people hunted animals in the nearby woods and planted small crops on their land. There were several different Native American groups living in this area when European settlers began arriving.

The Meadowcroft Rockshelter, located southwest of Pittsburgh, is one of North America's oldest archaeological sites. Archaeologists—scientists who study the remains of early human life—have found plant and animal remains, as well as proof that humans spent time near the shelter as early as 16,000 years ago. Visitors to the state can tour the site and learn about the lives of Pennsylvania's prehistoric people.

The Susquehannock made up the largest group of Native Americans in the area when Europeans arrived in the 1600s. The Susquehannock people were the first Native Americans in the region to make contact with the new settlers. The Susquehannock were very interested in setting up trade with the Europeans. They traded animal hides and other goods for European supplies such as cloth and tools. However, by the end of the 1600s there were only a few hundred Susquehannock left. Many died during wars with other Native American groups. Others died from diseases brought by the European settlers.

The remaining members of the Susquehannock tribe moved farther west and lived along the Conestoga River. The Susquehannock who lived in this region were called the Conestoga. The Conestoga were craftspeople and farmers and lived peaceably with the neighboring colonists. But their numbers were few and continued to decrease as members of the tribe died or moved away. In 1763, all except two of the remaining Susquehannocks were killed by a group of angry white settlers. This group—known as the Paxton Boys—was angry with other Native American groups, but took their revenge on the Conestoga.

At the same time, other Native American groups such as the Iroquois, Lenni Lenape (or Delaware), and the Shawnee lived in the region. The Lenni Lenape had occupied the area

around the Delaware River on the eastern side of present-day Pennsylvania. They were pushed westward by European settlers and for a short time lived in the Alleghenies. After the Revolutionary War, the Pennsylvania Lenape moved to Ohio. Today, most of their descendants live in Oklahoma. Little is recorded about the Shawnee tribe that

An artist's illustration of Lappawinsoe, a Delaware chief who made treaties with European settlers.

lived in the Pennsylvania area. Historians do know that—like other Native American groups—the Shawnee were also driven off their land by Europeans. Many Shawnee eventually settled in Oklahoma.

The Europeans

Many historians believe that English captain John Smith was the first white man to visit the region that included present-day Pennsylvania. Smith sailed up the Susquehanna River and met with the Susquehannock people in 1608. A year later, the Dutch government hired Henry Hudson to sail to North America in search of a water route to Asia. Hudson sailed into Delaware Bay and claimed the surrounding land on behalf of the Dutch. Other Dutch explorers soon arrived and set up trading posts there, but they did not construct any permanent settlements.

In 1634, an expedition from Sweden arrived and claimed ownership of the region. They called the area Nya Sverige, which meant "New Sweden." Tinicum Island was named the capital of the new Swedish territory. (Today the land is part of Pennsylvania and is located in the Delaware River, southwest of present-day Philadelphia.) But many European nations wanted to own this land. In 1655, fights between the Dutch and the Swedish settlers broke out. The Dutch finally won full control and reclaimed it for their government.

Then in 1664, English settlers decided that they wanted the land and claimed the same area for the Duke of York. The English gained and maintained control of the region. Nearly twenty years later, the English King Charles II gave William Penn a portion of that land. This land later became Pennsylvania.

The Charter of Pennsylvania

William Penn was a Quaker—a member of a religious group called the Society of Friends. The Quakers were not treated well in England and Penn wanted to establish a new colony where Quakers—and others—could live peacefully. King Charles II owed money to Penn's father, and in 1681 repaid his debt by signing a land grant. This grant, called the Charter of Pennsylvania, gave Penn the right to establish a colony in North America.

Along with a group of settlers, Penn arrived in 1682. They established the colony of Pennsylvania, and Penn was appointed governor. (The name Pennsylvania means "Penn's woods.") Together with other settlers, Penn organized the local government using a constitution that he called the Frame of Government. This stated that people had a right to own their land and to govern themselves. (Self-governing was a new concept for

To ensure peace between Native Americans and new European settlers, William Penn established treaties with different native groups.

most Europeans, since many European countries at that time were ruled by kings and queens.) The state constitution was changed many times over the years, but the early version helped to establish this new colonial government. Penn also helped plan the city of Philadelphia. This city was central to Pennsylvania society, and to the all of the early colonies.

A keystone is a central stone in an arch. It holds the arch together. Pennsylvania is called the Keystone State because it was centrally located among the thirteen original colonies and later played an important role in holding together the newly formed nation.

Colonial Wars

The population of Pennsylvania continued to grow, but most of the new settlers lived in the area that is now eastern Pennsylvania. Westward expansion was limited by the thick forests, the mountains, and a lack of roads wide enough to allow the passage of horse-drawn wagons. But settlers did venture west in search of more land.

Both France and Britain wanted control of the land west of the established colonies, in spite of the fact that the land was already inhabited by Native Americans. French and British newcomers started settlements on that land. Both countries built military forts in the region. This included land that is now part of western Pennsylvania. From 1689 to 1763, France and England fought over land rights in a series of four wars. As the tensions between the French and British settlers grew, some Native American groups took sides with one or the other country. In 1754 the French and Indian War—the last of the four wars—was officially declared. One of the first battles of this war was fought at Fort Necessity, in Farmington. The French and Indian War lasted nine years. In the end, Britain won. As a

During the French and Indian War, British forces overtook the French Fort Duquesne, located near present-day Pittsburgh.

result, the British controlled land in Canada, a large amount of land between the colonies and the Mississippi River, and some land in what is now Florida.

By the mid-1700s, many colonists were unhappy with British control. These colonists did not like Britain's taxes and trade rules. They also wanted to become an independent nation and govern themselves. In 1774, representatives from the colonies met in Philadelphia for the First Continental Congress. Their anger with Britain was discussed and they decided that all of the colonies would no longer trade with Britain. By April 1775, the Revolutionary War had begun and colonists were fighting the British. A month after the start of the war, the Second

Continental Congress met in Philadelphia. They voted for independence from Britain and began signing the Declaration of Independence—a document declaring that the colonies deserved more rights and were no longer loyal to Britain.

Though colonial forces won some victories at the beginning

Pennsylvania is famous for the Liberty Bell. It was brought to Pennsylvania from England in 1752 and was to be used for the state house. The bell cracked and was melted down and recast. It was rung to announce important events such as the first reading of the Declaration of Independence and at the end of the Revolutionary War. Today the bell is on display in Philadelphia as a symbol of the country's freedom and liberty.

of the war, many had problems fighting the British. British military men were well trained and had spent years fighting in or preparing to fight in battles. Most colonial soldiers were craftsmen, farmers, or held other non-military jobs. Fighting and traveling from battle to battle was new to them. At first, these colonists did not have the same weapons or the skills to use them. Through hard work and determination, the colonial armies grew stronger and more skilled, but battles against the British were still very difficult to win.

A few major Revolutionary War battles occurred in Pennsylvania. In September 1777, General George Washington and his men battled British troops at the Battle of Brandywine. Washington's men were forced to retreat. Later that month, the British invaded Philadelphia and managed to take over the city.

This John Trumbull painting depicts the signing of the Declaration of Independence in Philadelphia in 1776.

Washington's forces again faced British troops near Philadelphia at the Battle of Germantown in October. The British forces won the battle, and the colonial army had to retreat.

The following winter months were difficult for many colonial troops. Starting in mid-December, Washington and his men stayed in Valley Forge, which was located northwest of Philadelphia. His army was cold, tired, and hungry. They did not have enough warm clothing, blankets, or food. During the winter at Valley Forge, many soldiers died from illness. Others deserted—or left—the army.

In February of 1778, conditions began to improve. More supplies were brought in. Baron Friedrich von Steuben, a

Baron von Steuben is shown training American soldiers during the difficult winter at Valley Forge.

military man from Prussia (part of which is now known as Germany), volunteered to help train Washington's men to fight the British. By spring of that year, they had regained their strength and confidence and continued to fight British forces. With help from France, the colonial armies made progress against the British. The British forces left Philadelphia in June.

It is said that General George Washington asked Philadelphia resident Betsy Ross to sew one of the first American flags in 1776 or 1777.

Fights between the British and the colonists continued through that year and beyond. The British had also found allies in some of the Native American groups. In July 1778, some Iroquois in the region joined with the British to fight groups of settlers living in eastern Pennsylvania. The area was known as the Wyoming Valley and is near present-day Wilkes-Barre. More than half of the settlers there were killed during the Wyoming Valley Massacre. In turn, colonial forces destroyed several Iroquois villages in the area.

The Revolutionary War officially ended in 1783 and the colonies became an independent nation, the United States of America. In Philadelphia a national constitution was written. In 1787, after much debate and many changes, the colonies began to ratify or approve it. Pennsylvania was the second to approve the Constitution and became a state on December 12, 1787.

Philadelphia served as the nation's capital from 1790 to 1800. The national government then moved to Washington, D.C.

The 1800s and 1900s

Pennsylvania continued to grow and prosper into the 1800s. More settlers came to make a living from the land. Cities flourished and farms thrived. Pennsylvania became important to industrial progress. Pennsylvania's steel mills, coal mines, and factories helped the state's economy. Pennsylvania was also well-known for its glass production. A large portion of the country's goods were manufactured in Pennsylvania.

In 1812 Harrisburg became the state's capital. Bounded on the west by the Susquehanna River, the city was an important trade center. The general assembly moved to Harrisburg and the capitol building and other structures were constructed.

Pennsylvania's waterways were important for the transportation of people and goods. Pennsylvania's first canal, the Conewago Canal, had been dug in 1797 on the west bank of the Susquehanna River. It allowed the pioneers to travel from York Haven to Columbia by water. More canal systems were established to improve travel and trade. In 1825, the Schuylkill Canal, which connected Philadelphia and Reading, became the first long canal in the United States. Then in 1834, the Pennsylvania Canal opened, which allowed a passage over the Alleghenies. A series of large floods eventually destroyed many of the canals, but a portion of the Pennsylvania Canal has been restored and stretches between Raubsville and Easton. Railroads were expanded in the state in the 1850s, further improving the way Pennsylvania's goods were shipped.

From colonial times into the 1800s, many Pennsylvanians owned slaves. But when slavery was outlawed in the state, Pennsylvania became one of the many safe places for freed or escaped slaves to start new lives. The Underground Railroad was a route that slaves from the South took to gain their freedom in the northern states where slavery was illegal. People who were opposed to slavery led the slaves through this "railroad" at night. Some stops along this system were in Pennsylvania and many residents took part in helping the slaves. Historians estimate that more than 100,000 people tried to leave the South through the Underground Railroad. Not all attempts were successful and many died along the way. Others were caught and taken back to their masters. But many managed to escape to freedom. The borough (a community similar to a town or city) of Columbia, along the Susquehanna River in Lancaster County, became a popular place for runaway slaves to settle.

The slavery issue was one of the reasons why the Civil War began in 1861. Several southern states seceded—or separated— from the United States. They formed the Confederate States of America. Pennsylvania remained a part of the United States, which was also called the Union. The state sent almost 400,000 soldiers

Many African Americans fought for the Union during the Civil War. This troop poses for an artist at Camp William Penn in Philadelphia.

to fight the Confederate Army. State residents sent supplies and food to the Union troops. Pennsylvania also produced much of the military equipment that was used.

Confederate and Union forces fought many bloody battles throughout the North and South. In 1863, one of the most famous battles of the Civil War was fought in Gettysburg, Pennsylvania. The Battle of Gettysburg lasted from July 1 through July 3. More than 50,000 soldiers were wounded or killed, making it one of the bloodiest battles in history. Gettysburg marked the northernmost point that the Confederate Army reached. The Union Army defeated the Confederate Army, and forced them to retreat. President Abraham Lincoln delivered his famous Gettysburg Address on the battlefield in 1863, honoring those who had fought and died for the country and its freedoms. The South eventually surrendered to the North in

For three days, Confederate troops lead by General Robert E. Lee and Union troops lead by General George G. Meade clashed on the Gettysburg battlefield.

1865 and the war ended. The Confederate states rejoined the United States and the country worked toward rebuilding and reuniting.

Through the end of the 1800s Pennsylvania's economy continued to thrive. Jobs were plentiful, and people from the war-torn southern states as well as immigrants from Scotland, Ireland, Russia, and east European countries came to Pennsylvania in hopes of making a better life. Work in the factories and mines, however, proved dangerous and did not provide as much money as the workers had expected. In the late 1800s, many of these workers demanded better pay and safer working conditions. Some of the first labor unions formed in Pennsylvania. These unions were groups of workers who banded together to demand better conditions and better pay.

At this 1902 labor strike, youths protested the terrible working conditions forced upon young Pennsylvanians who worked in the factories and mines.

The 1900s

Pennsylvania continued to be one of the leading industrial states in the twentieth century. Unfortunately, in 1929 the Great Depression started, causing massive unemployment. Like many other states, Pennsylvania was hit hard. At one point almost 80 percent of the employees of steel mills and in the railroad business lost their jobs. Since these were two of the biggest industries in Pennsylvania, this meant that many people living in the state were unemployed. Without jobs, these workers had no money to feed their families or keep their homes. Nobody could afford to buy many products so the merchants and farmers who provided these products to the public also suffered. Many people were forced to leave the state in search of some form of income.

In 1940 the Pennsylvania Turnpike was completed. This was the country's first high-speed, multi-lane highway. The turnpike served as a model for most of the country's modern superhighways.

The state and national governments set up programs to help. Workers were employed to build and fix bridges, highways, and dams. Others were paid to work in the forests. Starting in 1939, World War II also helped the economy. As in World War I, more then twenty years before, the state sent many soldiers to serve in the military. Pennsylvania also provided supplies for the war effort. Workers were hired to operate the steel mills, factories, and coal mines. However, after the war, the demand for steel and coal declined, and many factories were shut down. It took many years, but the state's economy eventually bounced back and residents once again began to see profits.

Pennsylvania Today

Together with their state government, Pennsylvania citizens work hard to maintain their state. They respect the environment and have made efforts to conserve land and water. Pollution from factories and mills has been reduced and strict laws are in place to protect the environment. As a result, the forests are growing stronger, and many of the creatures that live in them are thriving. Lake Erie, which was once declared a dead lake, has been revived. Today it is a lot cleaner and healthier than it was thirty years ago. The state has also worked hard to preserve its history. Pennsylvania is home to many historic sites and landmarks. Residents and visitors alike are able to experience the state's history and appreciate the important role that Pennsylvania played—and continues to play—in creating and supporting the country.

Important Dates

14,000-8000 B.C.E. Early native peoples live and travel through the region.

1500 C.E. Native American culture flourishes in the Susquehanna River area.

1633-1674 The Dutch, Swedish, and English establish the first European settlements in the region that now includes Pennsylvania.

1682 William Penn and fellow settlers establish the colony of Pennsylvania.

1689-1763 A series of four wars between Britain and France occurs in the colonies.

1698 The colonies' first public school is opened in Philadelphia.

1752 The original Liberty Bell arrives from England, a small crack appears, and the bell is recast.

William Penn

1754 The French and Indian War starts in western Pennsylvania.

1776 The Declaration of Independence is adopted in Philadelphia.

1787 The Constitution of the United States is created.

1787 The country's first workable steamboat is used near Philadelphia on the Delaware River.

1790-1800 Philadelphia serves as the capital of the United States.

1811 The first steamboat to travel on the Mississippi and Ohio Rivers is launched from Pittsburgh.

1812 Harrisburg becomes the new state capital.

1852 The Pennsylvania Railroad is completed, connecting Philadelphia and Pittsburgh.

The Liberty Bell

1869 Uriah S. Stephens helps create the first national labor union, the Knights of Labor.

1940 The Pennsylvania Turnpike opens.

1946 The world's first computer, ENIAC, is created at the University of Pennsylvania.

1957 The first U.S. full-scale nuclear energy plant goes into service in Shippingport.

1979 An accident at the Three-Mile-Island nuclear power plant causes widespread concern.

1988 Sophie Masloff serves as Pittsburgh's first female mayor.

2001 Hijacked United Flight 93 crashes in a field in Somerset on September 11.

2003 A new pavilion for the Liberty Bell is built in Philadelphia.

3 The People

In 1790 the population of Pennsylvania was almost 435,000. Sixty years later, the number of people living in Pennsylvania dramatically increased to more than two million. The number of residents continued to grow rapidly through the centuries. In 2000 the official U.S. Census showed that Pennsylvania had a population of more than twelve million people. The people of Pennsylvania come from a wide variety of different cultures.

The First Residents

Native Americans lived on the land that is now Pennsylvania long before the first Europeans arrived. The Iroquois, Susquehannock, Shawnee, and Lenni Lenape in the region hunted, farmed, and lived on the land for centuries. Loss of land and hunting grounds, European settlement, and diseases brought by the Europeans decreased the Native American populations in the region.

The 2000 U.S. Census states that only 0.1 percent of the state's population is Native American. Today there are no federally recognized Native American reservations in Pennsylvania.

Bright-colored costumes mark the annual New Year's Mummers Parade in Philadelphia.

Native Americans dance at a powwow during a festival in Fairmount Park.

But many Native Americans from different tribes and nations live in the state. Native American Pennsylvanians own farms, have jobs in towns and cities, and hold office in local and state governments. Throughout the year, festivals and powwows (Native American dance celebrations) take place across the state. Pennsylvania also has many Native American historical landmarks and museums.

The Pennsylvania Dutch

The Mennonites, the Brethren, and the Amish make up a group of people commonly called the Pennsylvania Dutch. The name Pennsylvania Dutch comes from Pennsylvania Deutsch, which refers to German-speaking Mennonite immigrants. The ancestors of many of the Pennsylvania Dutch began coming to Pennsylvania in the seventeenth century. Many wanted to get away from the wars in Europe and find religious freedom in a new land. By 1775, the Pennsylvania Dutch made up one-third of the colony's population.

Today there are approximately 25,000 Pennsylvania Dutch people living in the Lancaster area. Some have adopted some modern ways of life. However, the lives of many of the Pennsylvania Dutch have not changed much from the lives of their ancestors. Many present-day Pennsylvania Dutch do not believe in modern conveniences such as electricity, telephones, or cars. Their farms are run in nearly the same manner as the farms of their eighteenth-century ancestors. Dutch farms can be seen alongside modern-day farms run by non-Dutch. On some Pennsylvania roads, you might spot Dutch horse-drawn carriages driven alongside cars. But not all Pennsylvania Dutch live on farms in eighteenth-century conditions. Some people of Pennsylvania Dutch descent live and work in cities and suburbs, using modern technology and conveniences.

Lancaster County in southeastern Pennsylvania is home to the second-largest population of Amish people in the world. In this county, and in other parts of the state, people can visit museums and historic farmhouses that share the history and culture of the Pennsylvania Dutch.

Amish schoolchildren in Lancaster County walk to their one-room schoolhouse.

Painting a Pennsylvania Dutch Tile

The Pennsylvania Dutch brought colorful good luck signs—sometimes called hex signs—to their new homes. They believed that special symbols such as birds, hearts, stars, flowers, and fruit brought good luck. Colors also had meaning—red for love, blue for truth, yellow for life, and green for good fortune and happiness.

Materials you will need:

1 white ceramic tile—4 inches by 4 inches (found in hardware stores)
Paintbrushes
Glass and tile paint (found at craft stores) in red, blue, and yellow
1 sheet of felt (at least 8 inches by 11 inches)
Craft or Tacky glue
1 piece of light cardboard (an empty cereal box, or the back of a writing pad)
Scotch tape
Newspaper

To make the stencil:

Draw your design on the cardboard. You can draw a simple bird, a pineapple, hearts, flowers, or a combination of some or all of these. Make sure that your design will fit on the tile. Cut out the design. Ask an adult to help if the cardboard is too

hard to cut. Throw away the cut-outs and keep the sheet of cardboard with the open spaces.

To paint the tile:

Spread newspaper to protect your work surface. Tape the stencil (piece of cardboard) to the tile. Brush different colors of paint over the different holes in the cardboard. (You can combine the yellow and blue paint to make green paint.) Paint the lighter colors first, then the darker ones. If you make a mistake, you can wipe the wet paint off with a damp piece of paper towel. When you are done painting, keep your stencil taped to the tile and allow the tile to dry for about a half hour. Make sure the paint is dry before lifting the stencil. If you find a mistake after you remove the stencil, you can gently scratch the unwanted paint off with your fingernail.

Let the tile air dry for several hours. When the tile is dry, cut a piece of felt and glue it to the back of the tile. You can use the tile as a paperweight, coaster, or as a decorative piece for your home.

A Mix of Cultures

According to the Census taken in 2000, Pennsylvania's population is about 84 percent Caucasian—or white. Most of these people have European heritage. Some are descended from the early European settlers: the Dutch, the Swedish, or the English. Other white residents can trace their ancestors to the Polish,

Young girls hold candles during a traditional holiday festival held at a Swedish church.

Italian, Irish, and Scottish immigrants who came to the state between the late 1700s and the 1900s. New European immigrants and Americans with European backgrounds continue to make Pennsylvania their home. Some come from foreign nations while many have moved from other states.

Today African Americans make up the largest ethnic minority in the state. Approximately 10 percent of the population is African American. In 1859, when the slaves in Pennsylvania were freed, many chose to live and work in and around Philadelphia and other Pennsylvania cities. Many of their descendants have made Pennsylvania their home today. After the World Wars, many African Americans from the south settled in the eastern part of the state. By 1944, almost 5 percent of the state's population was African American. Other African Americans may have moved to the state from other regions of the United States. Pennsylvanians of African American descent are active in the state's economy, communities, and local and state governments.

Young Pennsylvanians take part in a ballet class at the Philadelphia School of Performing Arts Charter School.

Famous Pennsylvanians

James Buchanan:
United States President

Buchanan, the fifteenth president of the United States, was born in 1791 in Franklin County. His family lived in a log cabin at a frontier outpost in Cove Gap but later moved to Mercersburg. Before becoming president, Buchanan was a U.S. congressman and senator. He also served as a minister to Russia and Great Britain (which meant he handled foreign affairs between the United States and these countries), as ambassador to Great Britain, and as secretary of state under President James K. Polk.
Buchanan was president from 1857 to 1861.

Reggie Jackson: ## Baseball Player

Reggie Jackson was born in Wyncote in 1946. A talented athlete, Jackson played baseball for the Oakland A's, the New York Yankees, and the Los Angeles Angels. His lifelong batting average was an impressive .490 and he hit 563 home runs during his career. Jackson was inducted into the National Baseball Hall of Fame in 1993.

Bill Cosby: ## Actor and Comedian

Cosby was born in Philadelphia in 1937. As an African American comedian and actor Cosby has been able to overcome prejudice and bring attention to the similarities—rather than the differences—among people of different backgrounds. Cosby has worked on many television shows for adults and children. In 1998, he was honored at the Kennedy Center in Washington, D.C., for a lifetime achievement in the arts.

Rachel Carson: Environmentalist

Carson was born in 1907 on a farm in Springdale and throughout her youth, was curious about nature. Carson was a very good writer and published her first magazine article when she was in the fourth grade. Carson's main concerns were studying, preserving, and protecting the environment and sharing her findings with the public. One of her books, Silent Spring *pointed out the health dangers of pesticides. She was one of the first people to call attention to how those chemicals pollute the land and water.*

Benjamin Franklin: Statesman and Scientist

Franklin was born in Boston in 1706, but moved to Philadelphia when he was seventeen. Despite having only two years of formal education, Franklin was a printer, author, inventor, scientist, educator, politician, and diplomat. He is well-known for using a kite to prove that lightning and electricity are related. Franklin is called one of the founding fathers of the nation because he had an important role in drafting the Declaration of Independence and the Constitution.

Fred Rogers: Children's Television Host

Mr. Rogers—as he was known to millions of people— was born in Latrobe in 1928, but lived most of his adult life in Pittsburgh. The first nationally broadcast episode of his television series, Mr. Rogers' Neighborhood, *aired in 1968. The show has been on television for more than thirty years, and has won four Emmy Awards. For his work with children, he was honored with the Presidential Medal of Freedom in 2002. Mr. Rogers passed away in 2003.*

49

Today almost 130,000 Hispanic people live in Pennsylvania. Many are from Puerto Rico. Hispanics started moving to the state in the 1920s. Some came as experienced farmers and found work in agriculture. Others found jobs in different lines of work and many opened their own businesses. During the last ten years, the Hispanic population has grown to include people from Mexico, Cuba, and the Dominican Republic. In many of Pennsylvania's cities, you can find businesses, restaurants, and stores owned by Hispanic Americans. Throughout the year in different parts of Pennsylvania, residents hold festivals and other events celebrating Hispanic and Latino culture.

Asians and Asian Americans make up a little less than 2 percent of the state's population. The state's Asian population includes Chinese, Japanese, Filipinos, Vietnamese, and Cambodians. Some of these people are the children or grandchildren of

Indian-American children practice their drums at a Hindu temple in Saylorsburg.

Families from all cultures and different walks of life have made the state their home.

immigrants who came to the state many years ago. Others are new residents. Regardless of how long they have lived in the state, their influence can be seen in different parts of Pennsylvania.

Philadelphia has a thriving Chinatown. This part of the city was started by Chinese immigrants who arrived more than one hundred years ago. Throughout the year visitors and residents go to Chinatown to shop at the stores, eat at the restaurants, or join in the cultural celebrations and holidays.

Historically Pennsylvania has always been known as a place where many people from different backgrounds and cultures gathered. Through the years the makeup of these groups has changed. But this diversity has made Pennsylvania into the appealing state that it is today.

Calendar of Events

Mummers Parade

On the first day of January, Philadelphia holds its internationally famous Mummers Parade. This is a celebration of clowns, fancy costumes, dancing, and music. String bands provide the music, but everyone—including the crowds—is invited to do the Mummers Strut, a comical squat-kneed dance.

Dog Sledding at Camp Brule

In February the cold, snow-covered mountains at Camp Brule offer the perfect setting for dogsled races. Spectators cheer for their favorite team, while enjoying a day of ice-skating, or participating in the ice-sculpting contest.

A musician at the Mummers Day Parade

Maple Syrup Festival

This festival is held in March in Erie's Asbury Woods. Visitors learn about making syrup, from the tapping of the trees to the boiling of the sap. Afterward many enjoy a hearty breakfast of pancakes topped with freshly made pure maple syrup.

International Science and Technology Festival

Pittsburgh offers its annual International Science and Technology Festival every April at the Carnegie Science Center. One-of-a-kind cars and musical instruments are displayed alongside other cutting-edge advances in technology. Visitors can sign up for hands-on workshops to discover what the future of science might be.

Devon Horse Show and Country Fair

This May event is the largest horse show of multi-breed horses in the United States. Located outside of Philadelphia, the fair offers a chance to watch children and adults run and jump their horses through a challenging course.

Elfreth's Alley Fete Days

Elfreth's Alley in Philadelphia claims to be the oldest residential street in the United States. During this colonial festival in June people can walk through the historic houses and be greeted by people dressed in colonial costumes.

Gettysburg Civil War Heritage Days

Over the course of a few days in July, visitors can see Civil War reenactments of the Battle of Gettysburg. Historians discuss the history of the battle and the war. The event also has a fireworks display and other entertainment.

A Civil War reenactment

Native American Festival in Airville

Every September a Native American festival is held at the Indian Steps Museum in Airville. This museum is located west of Philadelphia and houses one of Pennsylvania's largest collections of Native American artifacts. These include arrowheads and tomahawks. One of the festival's highlights is a powwow, a celebration of Native dances.

Train Display at Westmoreland Museum of Art

In November this museum in Greensburg sets up a dazzling display of antique toys and trains. Train enthusiasts can enjoy the twenty-eight feet of track laid out for the museum's eight trains.

4 **How It Works**

Though Pennsylvania is considered one of the fifty states, it is technically a commonwealth. The word commonwealth reflects the state's concern for the well-being of all of its citizens. Commonwealth or state, Pennsylvania has a system of state and local governments that help keep the state running.

Local Government

The state is divided into sixty-seven counties. A county is made up of several cities or smaller communities called townships. Each county has its own government, usually run by commissioners. These commissioners handle issues that affect the many communities within the county. But each city or township also has its own local government. Local officials are elected by the residents of the community. Most cities are run by mayors or city councils, which are groups of officials. Townships are often managed by selectmen, commissioners, or supervisors. City and township governments are designed to address local

> Three other states are also commonwealths. They are Kentucky, Massachusetts, and Virginia.

Built to be used as the Pennsylvania State House, Independence Hall in Philadelphia served as a meeting place for the Continental Congress.

Harrisburg is home to many historic buildings. This mansion was built in the 1760s for John Harris, the founder of Harrisburg.

problems. Issues concerning local budgets, land use, or the public school system are managed by these small governments.

Pennsylvania residents are active in their governments. Besides serving as officials, many residents attend numerous meetings and hearings that address local problems. Several times a year each city or township votes on things such as the budget and the school system. Through their votes, local residents are able to control how their town is run.

State Government

The state government is responsible for issues that affect the state as a whole. The job of state officials includes drafting, approving, and enforcing laws; managing state budgets; and handling issues between Pennsylvania and other states and between Pennsylvania and the federal government.

Tinicum Island (in 1634), Philadephia (in 1683), and Lancaster (in 1799) served as Pennsylvania's capitals before Harrisburg became the state capital in 1812.

How a Bill Becomes a Law

The ideas behind laws can come from different places—sometimes from legislators and often from state residents. A state resident with an idea for a law can present it to his or her state representative or senator. A proposed law is called a bill. It takes only one senator or representative to help develop a proposed law into a

Branches of Government

Pennsylvania's state government is divided into three main branches, each with different responsibilities.

Executive The governor, who is elected to a four-year term, is the head of this branch. The governor's responsibilities include approving and vetoing bills and supervising the state budget. The executive branch also includes officials who work with the governor such as the lieutenant governor, attorney general, and state treasurer.

Legislative The legislative—or lawmaking—branch is the General Assembly. Two houses make up the General Assembly: the senate and the house of representatives. Senators serve four-year terms and representatives serve for two years. The number of both senators and representatives in the General Assembly is determined by the population of the state.

Judicial The judicial branch is responsible for making sure that laws are followed. The state Supreme Court heads this branch. This court has seven justices who are elected to ten-year terms. Lower courts, such as the appellate, superior, and commonwealth courts, each handle different types of cases based on the kind of crimes committed.

bill. But if more than one assembly member supports the bill, chances are greater that it will become a law. It is also helpful if citizens are made aware of the bill, so that they can ask their Assembly members to support it. Bills can cover a variety of topics. For example, one bill might increase taxes to help pay for road repairs. Another bill might add harsh punishments for people who commit very serious crimes. Other bills define people's jobs, such as the role of volunteer firefighters.

If you are curious about what bills are currently being considered in Pennsylvania, go to this Web site: http://www.legis.state.pa.us/cfdocs/legis/home/session.cfm This site lists all the bills that are on the floor (which means they are being discussed) of both the house and senate.

State legislators meet at the state capitol building in Harrisburg.

The General Assembly member takes the bill to the Legislative Reference Bureau. The bureau translates it into official legal language, making the bill ready for formal presentation. The bill is then given a name and number and is sent to a special committee. It is the job of the committee to decide if the bill should go to the senate and house of representatives to be voted on. The committee members make their decisions partly based on public opinion. They hold hearings to see how the public feels about the bill. If the committee finds that the public likes some of the ideas contained in the bill but not other parts of it, changes—or amendments—can be made. If the general public is not in favor of the bill, the committee can decide not to send it to the members of the General Assembly. When a bill is rejected by the public and by the committee and not sent on to the General Assembly, it is said that that the bill has "died in committee." However, if the committee concludes that the bill is worthy, they will send it to the General Assembly.

The bill is first presented in the house from which it originated. This means that if a state representative helped draft the bill, it is first presented in the house of representatives. If the bill came from a senator, then the presentation starts in the senate. The bill is introduced and then sent to a special committee within the house or senate. The committee carefully studies the bill. The committee then presents the bill to the rest of the house or senate and discussions begin. At this time, senators or representatives have a chance to change the bill by suggesting amendments. The assembly members then vote on the bill. If the bill is passed, then it moves on to the other half of the General Assembly. The same process is carried out.

A photograph from 1906 shows a House of Representatives meeting at the capitol in Harrisburg.

If both houses can agree on the final bill and any amendments that were made, it is passed to the governor.

The governor must review the bill and decide whether to approve it or veto—reject—it. If he or she approves, it is signed into law. A bill that is vetoed by the governor can still become a law. In order to do this, the bill must be supported by two-thirds of the General Assembly.

The state encourages its residents to take an active part in their government. Many hearings are open to the public. Pennsylvanians can voice their concerns and suggestions to their local and state legislators. Many state legislators invite their constituents—the name for the residents they represent—to visit them at the capitol to learn more about the state government and its processes.

To contact your state legislators go
to this site:
http://www.legis.state.pa.us
In the box labeled "Find Members By," type in your zip
code or your county. (Have an adult help you if you do not
know your zip code or county.) From there you will be able to
find the contact information for your senators
and representatives.

5 Making a Living

Agriculture, mining, manufacturing, and service are industries that help keep Pennsylvania's economy running. These industries provide goods and services used around the country and around the world. But these fields also provide employment for millions of Pennsylvanians.

From the Land

Since the state's early history, agriculture and other natural resources have played a large part in Pennsylvania's economy. The lumber industry was important to the state during the eighteenth and nineteenth centuries. Millions of trees were harvested for lumber. The wood was used to build homes, furniture, wagons, and tools. Sawmills and paper mills flourished in the state. Today, Pennsylvania's lumber industry is much smaller. The state now focuses more on forest conservation. Pennsylvania does, however, have many Christmas tree farms. These farms grow different types of pine trees to be used during the holidays.

A young Pennsylvanian picks tomatoes on his family's farm.

Recipe for Applesauce Cookies

To make these tasty treats you can use store-bought applesauce or make your own. Have an adult help you with the cutting and the cooking.

Ingredients:

1-1/2 cups applesauce*
1 egg
3/4 cup sugar
1 teaspoon cinnamon
1 teaspoon baking soda
2 cups flour
1/2 cup softened margarine
1 teaspoon baking powder

Have an adult help you preheat the oven to 350 degrees Fahrenheit. While the oven is heating, combine all of the ingredients together and mix well. Drop small spoonfuls of the batter onto a greased cookie sheet. Bake the cookies for about 15 minutes or until they are a golden-brown color. When they are done, carefully remove the cookies and place them on a cooling rack. Be very careful because they will be hot. Once the cookies are cool, grab a glass of milk and dig in!

*To make your own applesauce, have an adult help you with the following instructions. Peel, core, and slice six medium apples. Place the small apple slices into a pan with 1 cup of water. Simmer the mixture for about fifteen minutes and stir in 1/4 cup sugar and a few sprinkles of cinnamon. Take the applesauce off the stove and let it cool. Once it is cool, you can eat it straight from a bowl or use it for your cookies!

Unlike the lumber industry, Pennsylvania's farm culture has remained steady throughout the centuries. More than one-fourth of Pennsylvania is farmland. Pennsylvania farmers harvest wheat, oats, mushrooms, soybeans, potatoes, and corn. Acres of farms are also dedicated to apple orchards. Farmers in the southern part of the state grow tomatoes, grapes, peaches, and strawberries.

Edible plants are not the only money-making crops. Businesses from around the country buy plants grown in Pennsylvania. These include cut flowers, shrubs, and ornamental trees.

Ranches around the state also raise and sell livestock. Hogs, sheep, and poultry are shipped around the state and around the country. On many eastern and southeastern Pennsylvania fields you might find herds of beef cattle grazing peacefully. Cows are also important to the dairy industry. Milk is one of Pennsylvania's top agricultural products.

Some Pennsylvania farmers raise llamas. Their hair can be used for clothing and they can be trained to guard sheep herds.

Pennsylvania land also yields mined products. Iron is mined from the land. Limestone quarries can be found in different parts of the state. This mineral is used for cement and other construction products. Many construction companies also use sand and gravel from the state. Different types of coal are mined in the state. Pennsylvania coal is used for processing iron ore, heating homes, and generating electricity at power plants. In 1859 the United States' first oil well was dug in Titusville. Oil continues to be an important product.

An aerial view of a mineral quarry.

Pennsylvania

Manufacturing

Pennsylvanians work in thousands of factories across the state. These factories manufacture goods such as food products, tools, and chemicals. The milk from the state's dairy farms is processed and made into a variety of foods. Pennsylvania food processing plants use the state's farm produce to make cookies, cakes, crackers, bread, and other treats. Medicines made in the state's factories also bring in money for the economy. Products such as industrial machinery, paints, tools, and electronics are also made by Pennsylvania workers.

Factories that manufacture and distribute steel have long been important to the economy. Iron mined from the land was used in steel plants across the state. The steel was used to build miles of railroad tracks laid down throughout the country. The framework for many buildings and skyscrapers also came from Pennsylvania's steel mills.

In one of the Hershey factories, a worker monitors Hershey Kisses as they move along a conveyer belt.

The Conestoga wagon was one of Pennsylvania's first manufactured items. With a high-arched canvas top and rear wheels almost six feet tall, these wagons were first produced in the Conestoga Valley in Lancaster County by the Pennsylvania Dutch. Until the railroads became popular, these wagons were one of the main means of transporting goods in the East.

Service

Today the service industry leads economic activity in the state. Service industries include banks, health care facilities, and retail stores. Three-fourths of Pennsylvanians work in such businesses throughout the state.

Tourism is an important part of the service industry. Millions of visitors come to Pennsylvania every year. Money that tourists spend on hotels, restaurants, and souvenirs is used to help the state's economy. The tourist industry also employs millions of Pennsylvanians.

Historic Pennsylvania draws tourists of all ages. Eager to learn about the state's and the country's history, many travel to Philadelphia to see the Liberty Bell, Independence Hall, and other colonial sites. Civil War enthusiasts often visit Gettysburg. Pennsylvania is also home to many museums and historical centers. Pittsburgh alone has four popular and well-respected museums: the Carnegie Museum of Natural History, the Carnegie Museum of Art, The Andy Warhol Museum, and the Carnegie Science Center.

The world's largest chocolate factory is located in Hershey, Pennsylvania. Milton Hershey, the founder of the company, built his factory in 1894, and the company has been making chocolate candies ever since. This chocolate industry was important to the state's economy and tourists still visit Hershey to learn about and sample these sweet treats. But Hershey visitors also spend time at the theme park, garden, wildlife park, and spa.

Professional sports are big in the state and Pennsylvania has seven teams in the professional leagues. State residents attend games, but these sports teams also attract visitors from

The Carnegie Museum of Natural History has a large collection of prehistoric fossils.

Making a Living

other states. Many major league baseball fans in Pennsylvania root for the Philadelphia Phillies or the Pittsburgh Pirates. When football season arrives in the fall, fans cheer for the Pittsburgh Steelers and the Philadelphia Eagles. The Philadelphia Flyers and Pittsburgh Penguins skate for Pennsylvania in the National Hockey League. Many fans spend a lot of tourist dollars during the sports seasons.

Fans of all ages root for their team at a minor league baseball game.

Pennsylvania

Many people of all ages enjoy the Pennsylvania slopes during ski season.

Making a Living

People are also drawn to Pennsylvania's wilderness. With at least two million acres of state forest and more than one hundred state parks, Pennsylvania is a haven for people who want to enjoy nature. Many families spend vacations amid the woods of the Poconos. The Delaware Water Gap National Recreation Area draws many visitors—particularly in the warm months. Pennsylvania truly has a lot to offer.

A hiker pauses to absorb the magnificent Pennsylvania landscape in Tioga County.

Pennsylvania's state coat of arms is represented on the state flag. On each side of the coat of arms is a horse rearing up on its hind legs. A bald eagle sits above with its wings wide open. The state motto—Virtue, Liberty, and Independence—is beneath the coat of arms. In the center of the coat of arms are the same three symbols present on the state seal: a ship, a plough, and three sheaves of wheat. Pennsylvania's state flag was officially adopted in 1799.

Pennsylvania's state seal, which was made official in 1791, shows a picture of a shield with the images of a sailing ship, a plough, and three sheaves of wheat. The ship stands for the commerce that developed by transporting goods by sea. The plough represents Pennsylvania's rich farmlands. The wheat represents the food, mineral resources, and other products that are produced in the state.

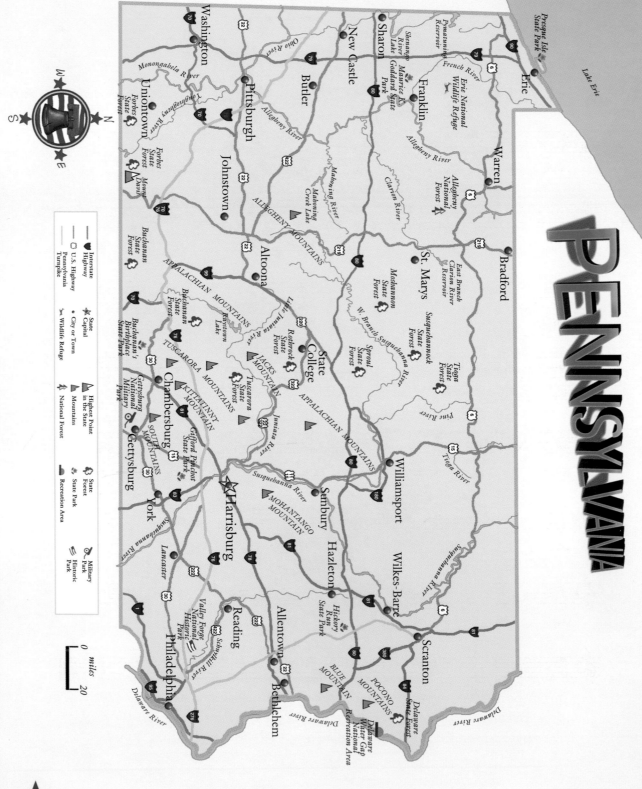

PENNSYLVANIA

Lake Erie

Presque Isle State Park

Erie

Warren

Bradford

Washington

New Castle

Sharon

Pymatuning Reservoir

Shenango River Lake

Maurice K. Goddard State Park

Franklin

French River

Erie National Wildlife Refuge

Butler

Ohio River

Allegheny River

Allegheny National Forest

East Branch Clarion River Reservoir

Clarion River

Pittsburgh

Monongahela River

Youghiogheny River

Uniontown

Forbes State Forest

Mount Davis

Forbes State Forest

Johnstown

Mahoning River

Mahoning Creek Lake

ALLEGHENY MOUNTAINS

St. Marys

Moshannon State Forest

Susquehannock State Forest

Tioga State Forest

W. Branch Susquehanna River

Sproul State Forest

Pine River

Williamsport

Susquehanna River

Tioga River

Altoona

APPALACHIAN MOUNTAINS

Buchanan State Forest

Raystown Lake

Rothrock State Forest

Little Juniata River

State College

Tuscarora State Forest

Juniata River

APPALACHIAN MOUNTAINS

Sunbury

Susquehanna River

Hazleton

Wilkes-Barre

TUSCARORA MOUNTAINS

Buchanan State Forest

JACKS MOUNTAIN

KITTATINNY MOUNTAIN

Gifford Pinchot State Park

Chambersburg

Buchanan's Birthplace State Park

Gettysburg National Military Park

SOUTH MOUNTAINS

Gettysburg

York

Harrisburg

MOHANTANGO MOUNTAIN

Hickory Run State Park

Scranton

Delaware State Forest

POCONO MOUNTAINS

Delaware Water Gap National Recreation Area

Delaware River

Lancaster

Reading

Schuylkill River

Valley Forge National Historic Park

Allentown

Bethlehem

BLUE MOUNTAIN

Philadelphia

Delaware River

Legend

Interstate Highway	State Capital	City or Town	Highest Point in the State	State Forest
U.S. Highway	Mountains	State Park	National Forest	Military Park
Pennsylvania Turnpike	Wildlife Refuge	Recreation Area		Historic Park

0 miles 20

W N S E

Pennsylvania

Words and Music by
Edward Khoury and Ronnie Bonner

PENN-SYL-VA-NIA, PENN-SYL-VA-NIA. Might-y is your name, Steeped in glo-ry and tra-di-tion Ob-ject of ac-claim, Where brave men fought the foe of free-dom, Ty-ran-ny de-cried, 'Til the bell of in-de-pend-ence filled the coun-try-side, PENN-SYL-VA-NIA, PENN-SYL-VA-NIA, May your fu-ture be filled with hon-or ev-er-last-ing as your his-to-ry.

State Song

77

More About Pennsylvania

Books About the State

Sherrow, Victoria. *Pennsylvania*. Farmington Hill, MI: Lucent Books, 2001.

Dolan, Edward F. *The Winter at Valley Forge*. New York: Benchmark Books, 2002.

Hess, Debra. *The Liberty Bell*. New York: Benchmark Books, 2004.

Seitz, Ruth Hoover and Blair Seitz. *Pennsylvania's Historic Places*. New York: Good Books, 1989.

Stein, Conrad. *The Underground Railroad*. New York: Children's Press, 1997.

Web sites

PAPowerPort—the Official State Web site:

http://www.state.pa.us

Pennsylvania State Park Kids Page:

http://www.dcnr.state.pa.us/stateparks/kids

Pennsylvania's Official Web Site for Travel and Tourism:

http://www.experiencepa.com/experiencepa/home.do

Valley Forge National Historic Park:

http://www.nps.gov/vafo/home.htm

About the Author

Joyce Hart, whose grandparents immigrated to Pennsylvania from Italy, has worked as an educator, an assistant librarian, an editor, and a desktop publisher. Currently she is a freelance writer and the author of four books. She has spent many years traveling the back roads of the United States.

Index

Page numbers in **boldface** are illustrations.